CHILLING Ice-Cream

Dear Reader

Do you lick an ice-cream slowly or eat it really quickly? Either way, it's delicious and fun.

There are many science secrets behind making ice-cream. Try some of the quick recipes in Chapters 2, 3 and 7.

> "NOT EVERYONE GETS ICE-CREAM HEADACHES. BUT IF YOU EAT ICE-CREAM TOO FAST, YOU MAY GET ONE."

In this book, you'll also find out how liquid nitrogen can be used to make smoother and fluffier ice-cream.

I hope you enjoy reading about ice-cream as much as I loved writing about one of my favourite treats!

Sharon Parsons

My sincere thanks to the following people for their time, information, images and enthusiasm for this book:

Naomi and the team at Subzero, Salt Lake City, USA.

Mark and the team at 7 Apples Gelato, Melbourne, Australia.

Dylan, Charlee, Tash and Jarrod, Melbourne, Australia.

NELSON
CENGAGE Learning™
For learning solutions, visit **cengage.com.au**

Contents

Chilling Ice-Cream

1 The Secret Ice-Cream Vault

Ice-Cream **Secrets** Inside!

Imagine it's your birthday and your party is at an ice-cream factory. You and your friends find a room with a huge ice-cream vault.

On the door is a sign:

Top Secret – Ice-Cream Vault

There is a huge padlock in the shape of an ice-cream cone. It stops you and your friends from opening the vault – until the key is found!

This book is like an ice-cream vault. You'll find some ice-cream secrets inside!

2 A Quick Ice-Cream Recipe

The **Secret** Behind **Quick** Ice-Cream!

The main ingredients needed to make ice-cream are not a secret. These are cream, milk, sugar and flavours.

What Is the Secret?

The secret to making quick ice-cream is science. If you know the science fact below, you can make quick ice-cream at home or at school.

SCIENCE FACT

Ice mixed with salt is colder than ice without salt. The salt dissolves into the icy water and lowers the water's freezing point. So it freezes at a lower temperature.

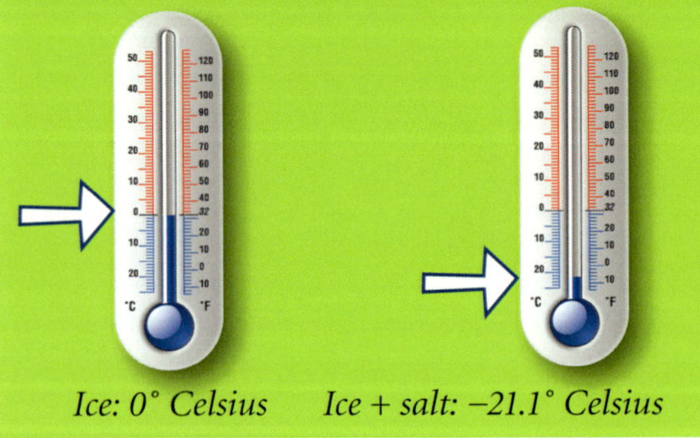

Ice: 0° Celsius *Ice + salt: –21.1° Celsius*

"Mmmm, my favourite!"

History and Technology

Who Invented the Ice-Cream Maker?

In 1846, Nancy Johnson, from the USA, was the first person to patent the hand-cranked ice-cream maker. It was a small ice-cream freezer with a handle to mix the ice-cream around. Her idea is still used by today's home ice-cream makers.

an ice-cream maker from the 1920s

An Ice Bath for a Quick Ice-Cream Recipe – Choc Chip

Before making the ice-cream recipe on pages 8 and 9, you'll need to make an ice bath.

Ingredients for the Ice Bath

- a large bowl, half-filled with crushed ice
- one cup of salt
- an extra half a cup of salt to add to the ice bath in Step 4 on page 9.
- a thermometer to test the temperature in the ice bath.

Making the Ice Bath

- Add one cup of salt to the large bowl of ice.
- Mix the salt and ice together with a wooden spoon.

Wait for five minutes. Put the thermometer in the ice bath. Is the temperature below zero degrees Celsius?

A Quick Ice-Cream Recipe – Choc Chip

Ingredients

- a third of a cup of cream
- two teaspoons of sugar
- half a teaspoon of vanilla essence
- one tablespoon of chocolate chips

Equipment

- a wooden spoon
- a small metal bowl

mixing the ingredients

How to Make the Ice-Cream

Step 1

- Put all the ice-cream ingredients into a metal bowl.
- Mix with a wooden spoon until the sugar dissolves.

Step 2

- Put the metal bowl into the ice-bath bowl (from page 7).
- Push the metal bowl down into the ice bath so that the ice is all around the outside of the metal bowl.

Do not get salty water in the ice-cream mixture!

A metal bowl sits in an ice bath.

Step 3

- Stir the ice-cream mixture for nine minutes.

Step 4

- Lift out the metal bowl.
- Add half a cup of salt to the ice bath and mix well.

Step 5

- Put the metal bowl back into the ice bath bowl.

Step 6

- Stir the ice-cream mixture for another three to four minutes.

Step 7

- Scrape the frozen ice-cream stuck to the bowl and mix it in, too. Stir until it looks like ice-cream.

Step 8

- Eat your choc-chip ice-cream!

Three friends could mix for three minutes each.

3 friends x 3 minutes = 9 minutes of mixing time

Again, three friends could take it in turns to stir the mixture for up to four minutes.

3 An Ice-Cream Experiment

The **Secret** of Making **Ice-Cream** in a **Bag**

Is it possible to make ice-cream in a bag?

Do this experiment with a friend and your teacher to see if it really works.

Step 1: putting the ingredients into the small ba

The Ice-Cream in a Bag Recipe

Small Bag Ingredients and Equipment

- one tablespoon of sugar
- half a teaspoon of vanilla essence
- half a cup of milk
- a **SMALL** plastic freezer bag that can be sealed
- a teaspoon
- a tablespoon
- a cup

Step 2: putting ice into the large bag

Large Bag Ingredients and Equipment

- crushed ice to half-fill the **LARGE** bag
- six tablespoons of salt
- a **LARGE** plastic freezer bag that can be sealed
- a tablespoon

How to Make the Ice-Cream

Step 3: the small bag goes into the large bag

Step 1 – Small Bag

Put these ingredients into the **SMALL** bag:

- one tablespoon of sugar
- half a teaspoon of vanilla essence
- half a cup of milk.

Seal the SMALL bag.

Step 2 – Large Bag

Put these ingredients into the **LARGE** bag:

- crushed ice to half-fill the **LARGE** bag
- six tablespoons of salt

Seal the LARGE bag and quickly shake it.

Step 3 – Small + Large Bag

- Open the **LARGE** bag and quickly put in the **SMALL** bag.
- Close the **LARGE** bag quickly.
- Shake the **LARGE** bag for five to ten minutes. Feel it to see when the ice-cream hardens.

Take turns at shaking the bag. It can get tiring!

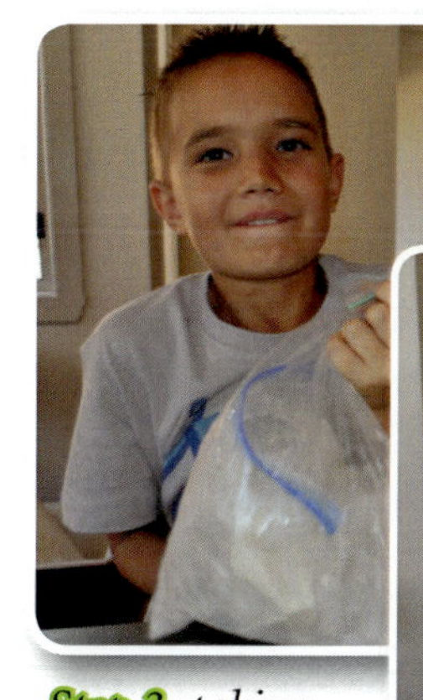

Step 3: taking turns at shaking the large bag

Step 4 – Open the Bags

- Open the **LARGE** bag and carefully remove the **SMALL** bag. Rinse off the salt water before opening it.
- Put the ice-cream into bowls and add chocolate topping.

Eat and enjoy!

Step 4: Ice-cream is ready to eat!

4 An Ice-Cream Headache

I Scream, You Scream, We All Scream for Ice-Cream!

An ice-cream headache happens when you eat very cold foods, such as ice-cream. When the food touches the roof of your mouth, your brain registers the cold as pain.

Does Everyone Get Ice-Cream Headaches?

Not everyone gets ice-cream headaches. But if you eat ice-cream too fast, you may get one.

How Long Can a Headache Last?

For some people, an ice-cream headache can last from a few seconds to five minutes.

Q Can you get an ice-cream headache in cold weather?

A It's impossible to get an ice-cream headache in cold weather.

How Can I Ease an Ice-Cream Headache?

Here are three things to try:

- Press your tongue to the roof of your mouth to warm it.
- Sip a warm drink slowly.
- Always see a doctor if a headache lasts for a long time.

Life Science

Most Popular Ice-Cream

The most popular ice-cream flavour is vanilla. Vanilla comes from a bean that grows on the Vanilla planifolia plant. The plant grows in places such as Madagascar and Mexico.

a vanilla plant

Social Studies

Second Most Popular Ice-Cream

Perhaps the second most popular ice-cream flavour is chocolate. And the most popular topping flavour for ice-cream is chocolate.

Yum, chocolate ice-cream!

5 Liquid Nitrogen Makes Better Ice-Cream

The Ice-Cream Science Show

"In today's show, you will find out why using liquid nitrogen results in the best ice-cream.

"For anyone at home, do not make ice-cream with liquid nitrogen. Leave it to the experts ... like me!"

Liquid Nitrogen Freezes Ice-Cream Quicker

"I've added liquid nitrogen to the ice-cream's ingredients but I have to stir it through quickly because it freezes the ice-cream almost immediately. Now, that's quicker than freezing ice-cream in a freezer!"

People who work with liquid nitrogen usually wear protective clothing, including goggles and gloves.

SCIENCE FACT

Nitrogen is an element usually found in gas form, but in order for it to become liquid nitrogen, it needs to be cooled down to about minus 200 degrees Celsius. That's colder than your freezer's temperature, which is about minus 15 degrees Celsius.

A Sub-Zero Ice-Cream Shop

"Enter this ice-cream shop and you will taste the smoothest ice-cream because they make ice-cream using liquid nitrogen. More about the shop very soon."

SAFETY FACT

Liquid nitrogen is so cold, it can cause serious injuries if comes into direct contact with the skin. It should only be used by people who have learnt how to use it safely.

Liquid Nitrogen Makes Smoother Ice-Cream

"The liquid nitrogen has made the ice-cream smoother, fluffier and creamier! That's because the ice-cream liquid freezes so quickly, the ice crystals do not have time to form, giving the ice-cream a very smooth, creamy texture."

Safety With Liquid Nitrogen

"An ice-cream shop in Salt Lake City, Utah, USA, uses liquid nitrogen to make their ice-cream. They store their liquid nitrogen safely inside a huge cylinder. The staff do not touch the liquid nitrogen, so there are no problems with safety."

SAFETY FACT

Liquid nitrogen must be stored properly at all times. It is dangerous because:

- you cannot see it
- you cannot smell it
- you cannot taste it.

serving ice-cream made with liquid nitrogen

SCIENCE FACT

Ice-cream made with liquid nitrogen is often called cryogenically frozen ice-cream. Cryogenics is the study of low temperatures.

Dr Sci-Ice-Cream Ends the Show

"We hope you enjoyed our show on how liquid nitrogen makes ice-cream smoother, fluffier, tastier and faster to make!

"Join us for next week's show when we make ice-cream monsters!"

SCIENCE FEATURE

Cryogenic Ice-Cream

Step inside an ice-cream shop where your ice-cream can be made within seconds! It all starts with a creamy liquid. Then you choose what you want added, like nuts or choc chips. Experienced staff add liquid nitrogen to the creamy liquid.

Want a Cryogenic Ice-Cream?

A Fast Procedure

1 Place an Order

Everyone, especially kids, LOVE the ice-cream made with liquid nitrogen.

2 Mix Ice-Cream

An experienced staff member finishes mixing the ice-cream with liquid nitrogen.

3 Put Ice-Cream in a Cone

After a few seconds of mixing, the ice-cream is ready to be put into the cup with waffle pieces.

4 Add a Final Scoop of Ice-Cream

The final scoop makes this ice-cream look really delicious!

5 See Happy Customers

Two happy customers will find out why this ice-cream is smoother, lighter and creamier than ice-creams made using traditional ways.

The owners of the store serve customers, too.

6 Italian Ice-Cream

Taste an Italian Gelato

Italy is famous for gelati and people around the world enjoy the taste. A gelato is usually made with milk – not cream. It has less milk fat and that allows the gelato flavours to stand out.

A Gelateria

Gelateria is the Italian word for a shop that sells gelati. Gelati is made with a mixture of ingredients and can be served in a cone (*cono*) or a cup (*coppa*).

Anyone for a gelato?

a gelateria in Melbourne, Australia

THE MOST POPULAR FLAVOUR IS FERRARO ROCHER – CHOCOLATE AND HAZELNUT!

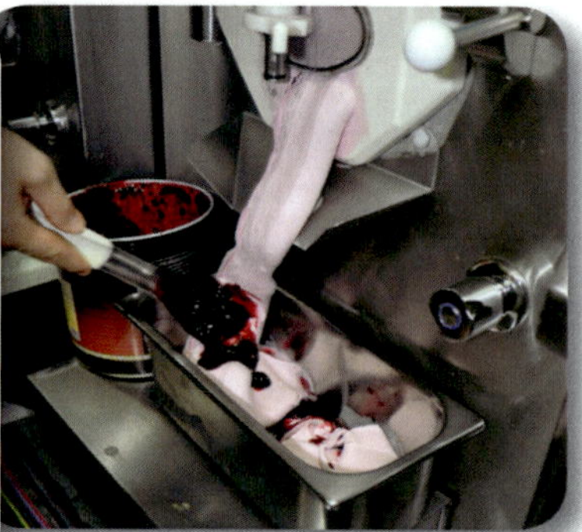

making gelati

Strawberry Gelato

Make this easy gelato recipe at home.

Ingredients

- 500 g of fresh strawberries
- 4 tablespoons of orange juice
- 175 g of caster sugar
- 450 mL of whipping cream

Equipment

- a fork
- a metal bowl
- a ceramic bowl
- a whisk
- a baking tin

Make the Gelato

1. In a ceramic bowl, mash the strawberries and mix to a smooth paste with the orange juice.
2. Stir in the caster sugar.
3. In the metal bowl, use the whisk to whip the cream until it thickens.
4. Stir the cream into the strawberry mixture.
5. Pour into the baking tin.
6. Freeze for one-and-a-half hours or until partly frozen.
7. Put the mixture into a clean bowl and break it up with a fork.
8. Whisk the mixture until smooth again.
9. Return the mixture to the baking tin. Freeze for at least five hours until frozen.
10. Put in the fridge for 30 minutes to soften. **Serve, eat and enjoy!**

GELATO OR GELATI?

Ask for one gelato, or ask for two or more gelati!

7 An Ice-Cream Recipe for Halloween

Celebrate **31 October** with Ice-Cream **Bats**

On 31 October, Halloween is celebrated by kids and families all over the world. Make this super-fast bat recipe!

Ice-Cream Bats for Halloween

This recipe makes two bats. You have to work fast – super fast – so the ice-cream doesn't melt! Are you ready? **GO!**

Ingredients

- two soft, sweet biscuits or wafers
- two large scoops of chocolate ice-cream
- some sweets for decoration, such as thin licorice straps and jellybeans